MAY - - 2018

Titanic's Last Hours

The Facts

by Meish Goldish

Consultant: Melinda E. Ratchford, EdD
Titanic Historian and Associate Professor
Sister Christine Beck Department of Education
Belmont Abbey College
Belmont, North Carolina

BEARPORT
PUBLISHING

New York, New York

Credits

Cover, Titanic Painting © Ken Marschall; 4–5, Titanic Painting © Ken Marschall; 5R, The Design Lab; 6, Titanic Painting © Ken Marschall; 7T, Wikimedia/tinyurl.com/y874s7ur/public domain; 7C, Wikimedia/tinyurl.com/y7jpbwej/public domain; 7B, © INTERFOTO/Alamy; 8L, © Chronicle/Alamy; 8R, Everett Historical/Shutterstock; 9, © Harland & Wolff Collection/National Museums NI/Mary Evans Picture Library Ltd/age fotostock; 10, Wikimedia/tinyurl.com/y7pgku49/public domain; 11, Titanic Painting © Ken Marschall; 12L, © The National Archives; 12–13, Titanic Painting © Ken Marschall; 14, Titanic Painting © Ken Marschall; 15T, © AF archive/Alamy; 15B, © Ann Ronan Picture Library Heritage Images/Newscom; 16, © The Print Collector/ Heritage-Images/The Image Works; 17L, © Macy's, Herald Square, New York City, c.1910 (b/w photo), Hall, G.P. & Son (1876–1914)/Collection of the New-York Historical Society, USA/George P. Hall & Son Photograph Collection/Bridgeman Images; 17R, Wikimedia/tinyurl.com/yavf7ss8/public domain; 18, © ZUMA Press, Inc./Alamy; 19, © Keystone Pictures USA/Alamy; 20–21, © Everett Historical/Shutterstock; 21TL, © Mary Evans/The National Archives, London. England/Mary Evans Picture Library Ltd/age footstock; 21TR, © Pictorial Press Ltd/Alamy; 22L, Library of Congress, 22TR, © Archive Pics/Alamy; 22BR, © Everett Historical/Shutterstock, 23T, © Paul Fearn/Alamy; 23BL, Library of Congress; 23BR, Library of Congress; 24, Titanic Painting © Ken Marschall; 25, © tc_2/Getty Images; 26–27, © Dorling Kindersley/Getty Images; 28–29, Bearport Publishing; 31, NARA/tinyurl.com/yc7v7lt4/public domain; 32, © Michael Rosskothen/Shutterstock.

Publisher: Kenn Goin
Creative Director: Spencer Brinker
Photo Research: Editorial Directions, Inc.

Library of Congress Cataloging-in-Publication Data

Names: Goldish, Meish, author.
Title: Titanic's last hours : the facts / by Meish Goldish.
Description: New York, New York : Bearport Publishing, 2018. | Series:
  Titanica | Includes bibliographical references and index.
Identifiers: LCCN 2017042961 (print) | LCCN 2017043830 (ebook) |
  ISBN 9781684024872 (ebook) | ISBN 9781684024292 (library)
Subjects: LCSH: Titanic (Steamship)—Chronology—Juvenile literature. |
  Shipwrecks—North Atlantic Ocean—Chronology—Juvenile literature.
Classification: LCC G530.T6 (ebook) | LCC G530.T6 G66 2018 (print) | DDC
  910.9163/4—dc23
LC record available at https://lccn.loc.gov/2017042961

For more information, write to Bearport Publishing Company, Inc., 45 West 21st Street, Suite 3B, New York, New York 10011. Printed in the United States of America.

10 9 8 7 6 5 4 3 2 1

CONTENTS

A SCARY SCRAPE

It was a dark, moonless night on April 14, 1912. The ship *Titanic* was sailing across the Atlantic Ocean from England to New York. At 11:40 PM, one of the ship's **lookouts**, Frederick Fleet, spotted a huge object in the water. "**Iceberg** right ahead!" he cried. The **crew** steered the ship sharply to the left to try to avoid the iceberg.

Within 40 seconds, the ship had curved left but still scraped against the giant mass of ice. Most passengers were asleep at the time, unaware that anything had happened. Others sensed the **collision**. Martha Stephenson, a passenger, said she heard "ripping and cutting noises." Another passenger, Mrs. J. Stuart White, said, "It was as though we went over a thousand marbles."

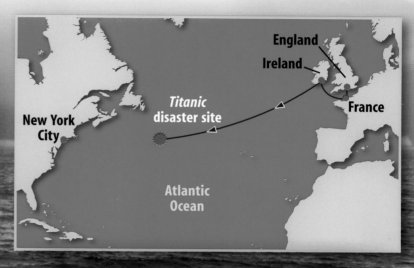

After leaving England, the *Titanic* made stops in France and Ireland before heading toward New York City. It hit the iceberg about 950 miles (1,529 km) from New York.

The *Titanic*, the largest ship in the world at the time, was on its very first **voyage**. It carried a little more than 2,200 passengers and crew members.

FACING A FLOOD

In the collision, the iceberg punched six openings about the size of two sidewalk squares in the right front side of the *Titanic*. Water immediately began to rush into the ship's bottom. It flooded the mail room and one of the **boiler** rooms. Fred Barrett, a boiler room worker, recalled, "A wave of green foam came tearing between the boilers, and I jumped for the escape ladder."

The bottom of the ship was divided into 16 **compartments**. After the collision, Ship Officer William Murdoch pulled a switch that automatically closed all the compartment doors. He wanted to stop the flood from spreading to other compartments. With water up to their waists, workers in the boiler and mail rooms rushed to escape before the closing doors could trap them inside.

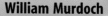

William Murdoch

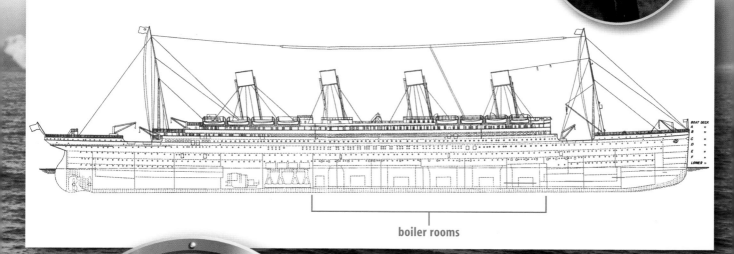

boiler rooms

The *Titanic* had six boiler rooms that held a total of 29 boilers. Workers shoveled **coal** into the boilers, where it was burned to provide power for the ship.

Workers in one of *Titanic's* boiler rooms

CHECKING THE DAMAGE

The crew told Captain Edward J. Smith that the *Titanic* had taken on water. Near midnight, Smith and the ship's builder, Thomas Andrews, went below **deck** to see how bad the damage was. They found that water had flooded two compartments and was quickly filling four more. The closed compartment doors weren't holding the water back.

Thomas Andrews

Captain Edward J. Smith

Most people had thought the *Titanic* was unsinkable. In truth, the ship could not float if more than four compartments were flooded.

Why were the compartment doors not doing their job? Unfortunately, they were too short. Once water filled a compartment, it simply flowed over the top of the door into the next compartment. The tremendous amount of water on board began to weigh down the front of the ship. Both Smith and Andrews were **horrified**. They realized that the *Titanic* would sink in just a few hours.

Door slides up to open

Titanic's compartment doors were not tall enough to reach the ceiling because the ship's builders never thought that water would rise that high. One of the doors is shown here.

PREPARING THE LIFEBOATS

At 12:05 AM, Captain Smith ordered crew members to uncover the lifeboats. They were stored on the ship's upper deck. The captain knew the *Titanic* did not have enough boats to save everyone. There were 20 boats in all, which could hold only about half of the more than 2,200 people on board. According to **maritime** law at the time, however, the *Titanic* carried an acceptable number of lifeboats.

This photo of the *Titanic*'s deck shows where some of the lifeboats were stored.

The *Titanic* could have held another 16 lifeboats. However, only 20 were on board because the ship's owners didn't want the boat deck to look crowded during the voyage.

The crew began to prepare the lifeboats. The plan seemed simple. After passengers got in a boat, it would be lowered by ropes 60 feet (18 m) down the side of the ship to the ocean. However, not all crew members knew what to do. Some had never had a practice **drill** with the lifeboats. Some didn't know which boats they were supposed to manage.

This illustration shows how lifeboats were lowered to the ocean by ropes.

CALLS FOR HELP

At 12:15 AM, Captain Smith ordered the *Titanic*'s **telegraph operators** to start sending emergency messages to other ships in the area. The messages read: "**C.Q.D.** We have struck an iceberg. Sinking fast. Come to our **assistance**." Three ships replied that they would come, but they were several hours away.

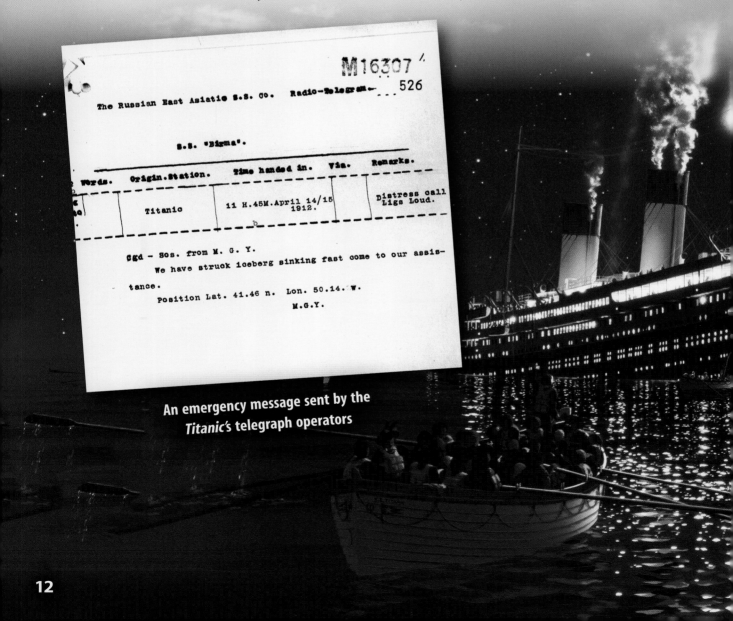

An emergency message sent by the *Titanic*'s telegraph operators

The closest ship in the area was the *Californian*. However, it never received *Titanic*'s message. Its only telegraph operator had gone to bed about 20 minutes before the *Titanic* sent out its alarm. At one point, the *Titanic*'s crew members spotted the lights of a ship—possibly the *Californian*—about 10 miles (16 km) away. They shot **flares** into the air to get the ship's attention. However, the "mystery ship" never came to the rescue.

The *Titanic*'s crew members fired rockets into the air to signal that the ship needed help.

It's possible that the unknown ship in the distance didn't approach the *Titanic* because it may have been blocked by icebergs or assumed that the *Titanic* was shooting off flares in celebration of its maiden, or first, voyage.

ALERTING PASSENGERS

By 12:25 AM, most passengers were still not aware of the danger they were in. Some children played on the boat deck, kicking small chunks of ice that had landed there during the collision. Crew members began telling passengers to put on **life jackets** and prepare to get into lifeboats. "Women and children first!" was the order. No men would be allowed to board, except for crew members who would row the lifeboats.

A painting showing crew members directing passengers to the huge boat deck

When the orders came, many passengers were asleep in their **cabins** and had to be awakened. Some got fully dressed before coming out into the cold night air. Others remained in their pajamas, simply throwing on a heavy coat. Some passengers refused to leave their rooms, believing they were in no danger. One traveler declared, "It will take more than an iceberg to get me out of bed!"

While passengers were told to put on life jackets, the ship's musicians began to play popular songs on deck to keep everyone calm.

A scene from a 1958 movie about the *Titanic* called *A Night to Remember* that shows the ship's musicians

Titanic crew members wearing life jackets

FILLING LIFEBOATS

At 12:45 AM, workers lowered the first lifeboat into the ocean. Some people were reluctant to board the small boats. Many passengers thought the giant ship *Titanic* was a much safer place to be than the small, wooden lifeboats. Only 27 people **occupied** the first boat, even though it could hold 65.

Crewmen helped women get into the lifeboats.

Some women insisted on staying on the ship with their husbands. The wealthy Ida Straus refused to leave her husband, Isidor. He owned Macy's, the world's largest department store. Ida told him, "Where you go, I go. As we have lived, so will we die together."

Isidor and Ida Straus

Isidor Straus begged his wife to get into a lifeboat, but she refused. She gave her expensive fur coat to her maid, who boarded a lifeboat. "I won't need this anymore," Ida told her.

Macy's department store in New York City in 1910

SINKING DEEPER

By 1:15 AM, the *Titanic*'s **bow** was tilted deeper into the ocean. All the passengers now realized the danger they faced and were eager to get into lifeboats. With time running out, the scene grew more **chaotic**. Crew members quickly began to toss women and children into boats.

This scene from the movie *A Night to Remember* (1958) shows both women and men desperately trying to board the *Titanic*'s lifeboats.

Some men were desperate to escape the sinking *Titanic*. One husband saw an empty seat in his wife's lifeboat and decided to join her. As the boat was being lowered, he leaped into it from the deck. Unfortunately, he landed on a passenger. In the fall, he broke two of her ribs and knocked her **unconscious**.

Some of the ship's officers used guns to fire warning shots to prevent men from rushing into the lifeboats.

In another scene from *A Night to Remember*, an officer on the *Titanic* fires a gun to scare men away from the lifeboats.

BRAVE WORKERS

By 1:50 AM, the *Titanic*'s bow was completely underwater. However, the ship's lights were still on because the engine room crew was working hard to keep the sinking ship from losing power. Lawrence Beesley, one of the passengers, noted, "To keep the engines going so that the decks might be lighted to the last moment, required **sublime** courage."

Engine workers kept the ship's lights on to help passengers and crew see their way around on deck.

Other crew members also showed amazing courage as the ship sank. Telegraph operators kept sending out **distress** messages. Officers loaded and lowered more lifeboats, sometimes giving their own life jackets to women or children who needed them. The *Titanic*'s musicians continued to play, even as it grew harder for them to stand on the slanted deck of the ship.

Radio Officer Jack Phillips

The *Titanic*'s radio station

Five ship mail clerks guarded the mailbags, which had been removed from the mail room when it flooded. About 3,400 bags containing approximately 7 million pieces of mail were lost in the sinking.

SAD GOODBYES

At 2:05 AM, the last two lifeboats were loaded and lowered into the water. Men said goodbye to their wives and children. John Jacob Astor IV, one of America's wealthiest men, helped his pregnant wife, Madeleine, into a lifeboat. Their son was born in New York City four months later.

Madeleine Astor

John Jacob Astor IV

The last lifeboats to leave the *Titanic* were overloaded with passengers.

Another millionaire on board, Benjamin Guggenheim, changed into his **tuxedo**. He told his servant, "We've dressed in our best and are prepared to go down like gentlemen." More than 1,500 passengers were left **stranded** on the ship. Some prayed. Some cried. Others just stood silently as the musicians continued to play.

Most women and children who traveled in first class escaped the *Titanic*. Those left behind were mostly third-class passengers who stayed in the ship's lower levels. They didn't make their way up to the boat deck in time to board the lifeboats.

Benjamin Guggenheim was a wealthy American businessman.

Third-class passengers Emily Goldsmith and her son, Frank Goldsmith Jr. (left), were able to board lifeboats and survived. Frank Goldsmith Sr. (right) unfortunately went down with the ship.

THE FINAL MINUTES

At 2:17 AM, *Titanic*'s lights began to **flicker** on and off. The musicians no longer played. Captain Smith ordered his crew to stop working. "Well, boys," he said. "Do your best for the women and children and look out for yourselves."

One **survivor** wrote, "I hung on by the rail and then let myself drop 75 feet (23 m) into the sea. When I hit the water, it was like a giant knife cutting into me. My limbs and body ached for days afterward."

The *Titanic* was now tilted at a **steep** angle. Many items fell from the ship into the ocean—from beds and pianos to tables, dishes, and suitcases. The ship's **stern** rose high into the air. Many people climbed to the top to stay as far away from the ocean as possible. Those who couldn't hold on fell into the freezing water. A few lucky ones managed to swim to lifeboats and climb inside.

As the back of the ship rose into the air, hundreds of passengers and crew fell into the ocean.

THE *TITANIC* DISAPPEARS

At 2:20 AM, the *Titanic* sank completely into the deep ocean. People in lifeboats watched in horror as the giant ship disappeared. Ruth Becker, a survivor, recalled that after the ship sank, "We heard the cries of hundreds of people struggling in the icy cold water, crying for help with a cry we knew could not be answered."

Eventually, the crying stopped. The people bobbing in the ocean could survive only about 30 minutes in the freezing water. With the rescue ship *Carpathia* still nearly two hours away, many soon died of **hypothermia**. Only the lucky 706 people in lifeboats survived.

Women bravely rowed some of the lifeboats. One famous *Titanic* survivor, Margaret "Molly" Brown, encouraged the women in her boat to row and to pick up swimmers from the ocean.

HOW THE *TITANIC* SANK

It took two hours and forty minutes for the *Titanic* to sink after hitting the iceberg. Here's how it happened, from beginning to end.

When the iceberg scraped against the *Titanic*, it punched several thin openings in the right front side of the ship.

After the scrape, the first five compartments quickly flooded.

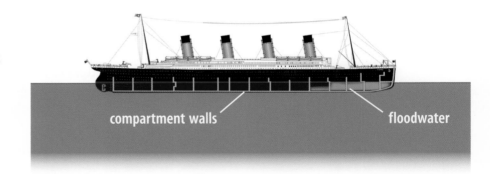

Water poured into the boat about 15 times faster than it could be pumped out. The ship began to sink.

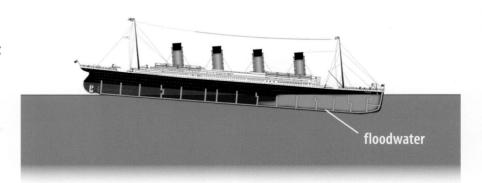

The weight of the incoming water caused the front of the ship to tilt downward into the ocean.

The back of the giant ship rose into the air at an angle. It placed great **stress** on the middle of the ship.

stress point

The ship broke into two pieces.

The front end of the *Titanic* sank to the bottom of the ocean first. After floating briefly, the back end of the ship sank as well.

Glossary

assistance (uh-SISS-tuhnss) help

boiler (BOI-lur) a tank that burns fuel in order to heat a building or other structure, such as a ship

bow (BOU) the front end of a ship

cabins (KAB-inz) small, private rooms where passengers and crew can sleep

chaotic (kay-OT-ik) in a state of total confusion

coal (KOHL) a black rocklike type of fossil fuel that is dug from the ground and can be burned to make electricity

collision (kuh-LIH-zhuhn) a crash

compartments (kuhm-PART-muhnts) separate sections of a container or ship

C.Q.D. (SEE-KYOO-DEE) one of the first distress signals used to radio for help; it means, "All stations: distress"

crew (KROO) a group of people who work together

deck (DEK) the floor of a ship or boat

distress (diss-TRESS) needing help

drill (DRIL) an exercise or activity that is practiced over and over

flares (FLAIRZ) torches that burn to create bright light

flicker (FLIK-uhr) shine unsteadily

horrified (HOR-uh-fide) shocked

hypothermia (hye-puh-THUR-mee-uh) a condition in which a person's body temperature has become dangerously low

iceberg (EYESS-berg) a large floating mass of ice in the ocean

life jackets (LIFE JAK-its) special vests that keep people afloat in water

lookouts (LUK-outs) people who keep watch

maritime (MER-i-tyme) having to do with the sea

occupied (OK-yuh-pide) lived in or sat in a place

steep (STEEP) having a sharp slope or slant

stern (STERN) the rear or back of a ship

stranded (STRAN-did) left helpless in a strange or dangerous place

stress (STRESS) pressure placed on an object

sublime (suh-BLIME) so excellent that it inspires great admiration

survivor (sur-VYE-vur) a person who lives through a disaster

telegraph operators (TEL-uh-graf OP-uh-ray-turz) people who sent messages over long distances using a code of electric signals

tuxedo (tuhk-SEE-doh) a man's suit worn for fancy occasions

unconscious (uhn-KON-shuhss) not able to see, feel, or think

voyage (VOI-ij) a long journey, often across an ocean

BIBLIOGRAPHY

Adams, Simon. *Eyewitness: Titanic.* New York: Dorling Kindersley (2014).

Hopkinson, Deborah. *Titanic: Voices from the Disaster.* New York: Scholastic (2014).

Tibballs, Geoff. *The Titanic: The Extraordinary Story of the Unsinkable Ship.* Pleasantville, NY: Reader's Digest (1998).

Yasuda, Anita. *The Sinking of the Titanic.* North Mankato, MN: ABDO (2013).

READ MORE

Blake, Kevin. *Titanic's Fatal Voyage (Titanica).* New York: Bearport (2018).

Brown, Don. *All Stations! Distress!* New York: Roaring Brook Press (2010).

Dubowski, Mark. *Titanic: The Disaster that Shocked the World!* New York: Dorling Kindersley (2015).

LEARN MORE ONLINE

To learn more about the *Titanic*'s last hours, visit
www.bearportpublishing.com/Titanica

INDEX

ABOUT THE AUTHOR

Meish Goldish has written more than 300 books for children. His book *Colonial Williamsburg* was named a Notable Social Studies Trade Book for Young People in 2017 by the National Council for the Social Studies and the Children's Book Council. He lives in Brooklyn, New York.